Foundations of Business

GEB 1011

Value Edition for Miami Dade College

Pride | Hughes | Kapoor

CENGAGE
Learning·

Australia • Brazil • Japan • Korea • Mexico • Singapore • Spain • United Kingdom • United States

CENGAGE
Learning·

Foundations of Business: GEB1011 Subtitle, Value Edition for Miami Dade College

Foundations of Business, Fourth Edition
Pride | Hughes | Kapoor

© 2015, 2013 Cengage Learning. All rights reserved.

Senior Manager, Student Engagement:
Linda deStefano

Manager, Student Engagement:
Julie Dierig

Marketing Manager:
Rachael Kloos

Manager, Premedia:
Kim Fry

Manager, Intellectual Property Project Manager:
Brian Methe

Senior Manager, Production:
Donna M. Brown

Manager, Production:
Terri Daley

For product information and technology assistance, contact us at
Cengage Learning Customer & Sales Support, 1-800-354-9706

For permission to use material from this text or product,
submit all requests online at **cengage.com/permissions**
Further permissions questions can be emailed to
permissionrequest@cengage.com

This book contains select works from existing Cengage Learning resources and was produced by Cengage Learning Custom Solutions for collegiate use. As such, those adopting and/or contributing to this work are responsible for editorial content accuracy, continuity and completeness.

Compilation © 2015 Cengage Learning

ISBN: 978-1-305-29350-2

WCN: 01-100-101

Cengage Learning
20 Channel Center Street
Boston, MA 02210
USA

Cengage Learning is a leading provider of customized learning solutions with office locations around the globe, including Singapore, the United Kingdom, Australia, Mexico, Brazil, and Japan. Locate your local office at:
www.international.cengage.com/region.

Cengage Learning products are represented in Canada by Nelson Education, Ltd.

For your lifelong learning solutions, visit **www.cengage.com/custom.**

Visit our corporate website at **www.cengage.com.**

Brief Contents

Part 1   The Environment of Business...1

Part 2   Business Ownership and Entrepreneurship 100

Part 3   Descriptive Statistics: Numerical Measures.............................. 85

Part 4   Introduction to Probability 148

Part 5   Discrete Probability Distributions 193

Part 6   Continuous Probability Distributions....................... 232

Answer Key, Glossary, Name Index, Subject Index

12 week Term, mini-term with project

12 week Term, mini-term

12 week Term, Spring

16 week Term, Fall Project

16 week Term, Spring

16 Week Term, Spring Project

Group Project

Word Match Pages, Chapters 1-16

Introduction to Business Chapter Quizzes

Contents

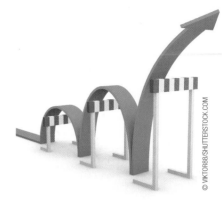

PART 1   The Environment of Business   1

Chapter 1: Exploring the World of Business and Economics   1

→ *Inside Business:* How Starbucks Brews Up Global Profits 2

Your Future in the Changing World of Business 3

Career Success: Improve Your Productivity! 4
Why Study Business? 4

Personal Apps: Sometimes you have to reach for success! 5
Special Note to Business Students, 7

Business: A Definition 8
The Organized Effort of Individuals, 8 ● Satisfying Needs, 9 ● Business Profit, 9

Types of Economic Systems 10

Entrepreneurial Success: Building a Million-Dollar App Business 12
Capitalism, 12 ● Capitalism in the United States, 13 ● Command Economies, 14

Measuring Economic Performance 15
The Importance of Productivity in the Global Marketplace, 15 ● The Nation's Gross Domestic Product, 16 ● Important Economic Indicators That Measure a Nation's Economy, 16

The Business Cycle 17

Types of Competition 19
Perfect Competition, 19

Personal Apps: Why do consumers choose one product instead of another? 21
Monopolistic Competition, 21 ● Oligopoly, 21 ● Monopoly, 22

American Business Today 22
Early Business Development, 22 ● Business Development in the 1900s, 23 ● A New Century: 2000 and Beyond, 24 ● The Current Business Environment, 24 ● The Challenges Ahead, 25

Summary 26

Key Terms 28

Discussion Questions 28

Test Yourself 28

Video Case: KlipTech Turns Recycled Paper into Products and Profits 30

Building Skills for Career Success 31

Endnotes 31

Chapter 2: Being Ethical and Socially Responsible   32

→ *Inside Business:* Chipotle Mexican Grill's "Food with Integrity" 33

Business Ethics Defined 34

Ethical Issues 34
Fairness and Honesty, 35 ● Organizational Relationships, 35

Personal Apps: In some buying situations, the "right" thing to do isn't always clear, is it? 35
Conflict of Interest, 36 ● Communications, 36

Factors Affecting Ethical Behavior 36
Individual Factors Affecting Ethics, 37 ● Social Factors Affecting Ethics, 37 ● "Opportunity" as a Factor Affecting Ethics, 38

Encouraging Ethical Behavior 38
Government's Role in Encouraging Ethics, 38 ● Trade Associations' Role in Encouraging Ethics, 39 ● Individual Companies' Role in Encouraging Ethics, 39

Social Responsibility 42

The Evolution of Social Responsibility in Business 44
Historical Evolution of Business Social Responsibility, 45

Two Views of Social Responsibility 46
The Economic Model, 46 ● The Socioeconomic Model, 47 ● The Pros and Cons of Social Responsibility, 47

Consumerism 48
The Six Basic Rights of Consumers, 48

Personal Apps: Do you always know what you're buying? 50
Major Consumerism Forces, 50

Employment Practices 50
Affirmative Action Programs, 52 ● Training Programs for the Hard-Core Unemployed, 53

Concern for the Environment 54
Effects of Environmental Legislation, 54

Sustain the Planet: Social Responsibility at Xerox 55

Entrepreneurial Success: Social Entrepreneurs of Tomorrow 57
Who Should Pay for a Clean Environment? 57

Implementing a Program of Social Responsibility 58
Developing a Program of Social Responsibility, 58 ● Funding the Program, 59

Summary 59

Key Terms 60

Discussion Questions 60

Test Yourself 61

Video Case: PortionPac Chemical Is People-Friendly, Planet-Friendly 62

Building Skills for Career Success 63

Endnotes 64

Chapter 3: Exploring Global Business 65

→ *Inside Business:* Coca-Cola 66

The Basis for International Business 67
Absolute and Comparative Advantage, 67 • Exporting and Importing, 68

Restrictions to International Business 70
Types of Trade Restrictions, 70 • Reasons for Trade Restrictions, 72

Personal Apps: What's your reaction when you see "Made in America" or "Made in the USA" on a product? 72
Reasons Against Trade Restrictions, 73

Career Success: The Global Economy Creates Jobs at Home, Too 73

The Extent of International Business 73
The World Economic Outlook for Trade, 74

International Trade Agreements 77
The General Agreement on Tariffs and Trade and the World Trade Organization, 77 • World Trade and the Global Economic Crisis, 78 • International Economic Organizations Working to Foster Trade, 78

Methods of Entering International Business 81
Licensing, 81 • Exporting, 82 • Joint Ventures, 83 • Totally Owned Facilities, 83

Striving for Success: Services Team Up to Enter India 84
Strategic Alliances, 84 • Trading Companies, 84 • Countertrade, 85 • Multinational Firms, 85

Sources of Export Assistance 86

Financing International Business 87
The Export-Import Bank of the United States, 87

Personal Apps: Do you know what a euro is worth? 88
Multilateral Development Banks, 88 • The International Monetary Fund, 88 • The Challenges Ahead, 89

Summary 90

Key Terms 91

Discussion Questions 91

Test Yourself 91

Video Case: Keeping Brazil's Economy Hot 93

Building Skills for Career Success 94

Running a Business: Part 1: Let's Go Get a Graeter's! 95

Building a Business Plan: Part 1 97

Endnotes 99

© ANDY DEAN PHOTOGRAPHY/SHUTTERSTOCK.COM

PART 2 Business Ownership and Entrepreneurship 100

Chapter 4: Choosing a Form of Business Ownership 100

→ *Inside Business:* Berkshire Hathaway Buys and Holds for Long-Term Growth 101

Sole Proprietorships 102
Advantages of Sole Proprietorships, 102 • Disadvantages of Sole Proprietorships, 104

Personal Apps: Do you dream of being your own boss? 104
Beyond the Sole Proprietorship, 105

Partnerships 105
Types of Partners, 105 • The Partnership Agreement, 106

Advantages and Disadvantages of Partnerships 106
Advantages of Partnerships, 106 • Disadvantages of Partnerships, 108 • Beyond the Partnership, 109

Corporations 109
Corporate Ownership, 110 • Forming a Corporation, 110

Personal Apps: Are you a stockholder? 111
Corporate Structure, 112

Ethical Success or Failure? Do We Need More Women in the Board Room? 113

Advantages and Disadvantages of Corporations 113
Advantages of Corporations, 114 • Disadvantages of Corporations, 114

Social Media: Going Social with SCORE 115

Special Types of Business Ownership 116
S-Corporations, 116 • Limited-Liability Companies, 116 • Not-for-Profit Corporations, 117

Joint Ventures and Syndicates 118
Joint Ventures, 118 • Syndicates, 118

Corporate Growth 119
Growth from Within, 119 • Growth Through Mergers and Acquisitions, 119 • Merger and Acquisition Trends for the Future, 121

Summary 121

Key Terms 123

Discussion Questions 123

Test Yourself 123

Video Case: AT&T and T-Mobile: What Went Wrong with Their Merger? 125

Building Skills for Career Success 125

Endnotes 126

Chapter 5: Small Business, Entrepreneurship, and Franchises 127

→ *Inside Business:* Dunkin' Brands Helps Franchisees Brew up Sales 128

Small Business: A Profile 128
The Small-Business Sector, 129 • Industries That Attract Small Businesses, 130

Personal Apps: Have you worked for a small business? 130

The People in Small Businesses: The Entrepreneurs 131
Characteristics of Entrepreneurs, 131 • Other Personal Factors, 131 • Motivation, 132 • Women as Small-Business Owners, 132 • Teenagers as Small-Business Owners, 133 • Why Some Entrepreneurs and Small Businesses Fail, 133

Career Success: Is Entrepreneurship in Your Future? 133

The Importance of Small Businesses in Our Economy 134
Providing Technical Innovation, 135 • Providing Employment, 136 • Providing Competition, 136 • Filling Needs of Society and Other Businesses, 136

The Pros and Cons of Smallness 136
Advantages of Small Business, 136 • Disadvantages of Small Business, 137

Entrepreneurial Success: Students by Day, Entrepreneurs by Night 138

The Importance of a Business Plan, 138 • Components of a Business Plan, 138

Personal Apps: A business plan is a great idea! 140

The Small Business Administration 141
SBA Management Assistance, 141 • Help for Minority-Owned Small Businesses, 142 • SBA Financial Assistance, 143

Franchising 144
What Is Franchising? 144 • Types of Franchising, 144

The Growth of Franchising 146
Are Franchises Successful? 147 • Advantages of Franchising, 147 • Disadvantages of Franchising, 148

Global Perspectives in Small Business 149

Summary 150

Key Terms 151

Discussion Questions 151

Test Yourself 151

Video Case: From Two Men and a Truck to 220 Franchises and 1,400 Trucks 153

Building Skills for Career Success 154

Running a Business: Part 2: Graeter's: A Fourth-Generation Family Business 155

Building a Business Plan: Part 2 157

Endnotes 158

PART 3 Management and Organization 159

Chapter 6: Understanding the Management Process 159

→ *Inside Business:* Amazon's Customer First Philosophy 160

What Is Management? 160

Personal Apps: Are you already a manager? 161

Basic Management Functions 162
Planning, 162

Career Success: Your Personal SWOT Analysis 164
Organizing the Enterprise, 165 • Leading and Motivating, 165 • Controlling Ongoing Activities, 166

Kinds of Managers 167
Levels of Management, 167 • Areas of Management Specialization, 168

Key Skills of Successful Managers 170
Conceptual Skills, 170 • Analytic Skills, 170 • Interpersonal Skills, 171 • Technical Skills, 171 • Communication Skills, 171

Social Media: CEO Dilemma: To Blog or Not to Blog? 171

Leadership 172
Formal and Informal Leadership, 172

Personal Apps: Who do you admire? 172
Styles of Leadership, 172 • Which Leadership Style Is the Best? 173

Managerial Decision Making 173
Identifying the Problem or Opportunity, 173 • Generating Alternatives, 174 • Selecting an Alternative, 174 • Implementing and Evaluating the Solution, 175

Managing Total Quality 175

Summary 176

Key Terms 177

Discussion Questions 177

Test Yourself 178

Video Case: L.L.Bean Relies on Its Core Values and Effective Leadership 179

Building Skills for Career Success 180

Endnotes 181

Chapter 7: Creating a Flexible Organization 183

→ *Inside Business:* Autonomy Fosters Innovation and Success at W.L. Gore 184

What Is an Organization? 185
Developing Organization Charts, 185 • Major Considerations for Organizing a Business, 185

Job Design 186
Job Specialization, 186 • The Rationale for Specialization, 187 • Alternatives to Job Specialization, 188

Departmentalization 188
By Function, 188 • By Product, 188 • By Location, 189 • By Customer, 189 • Combinations of Bases, 189

Delegation, Decentralization, and Centralization 190
Delegation of Authority, 190

Entrepreneurial Success: Successful Leaders Are Successful Delegators 191
Decentralization of Authority, 191

The Span of Management 192
Wide and Narrow Spans of Management, 192 • Organizational Height, 193

Forms of Organizational Structure 193
The Line Structure, 193

Personal Apps: Do you have a mentor? 194
The Line-and-Staff Structure, 194 • The Matrix Structure, 195 • The Network Structure, 196

Corporate Culture 197

Striving for Success: Dell Restructures to Jump-Start Innovation 198

Committees and Task Forces 199

The Informal Organization and the Grapevine 199

Personal Apps: Will you fit in? 200

Summary 200

Key Terms 201

Discussion Questions 202

Test Yourself 202

Video Case: Zappos Wants to Make Customers (and Employees) Happy 203

Building Skills for Career Success 204

Endnotes 205

Chapter 8: **Producing Quality Goods and Services 206**

→ **Inside Business:** Intel Invests in State-of-the-Art Production 207

What Is Production? 208
How American Manufacturers Compete in the Global Marketplace, 208

Entrepreneurial Success: Profit from Demand for "Made in America" 209
Careers in Operations Management, 210

The Conversion Process 210
Manufacturing Using a Conversion Process, 211

The Increasing Importance of Services 212
Planning Quality Services, 212 • Evaluating the Quality of a Firm's Services, 213

Where Do New Products and Services Come From? 213
Research and Development, 213

Personal Apps: Got a good idea? 214
Product Extension and Refinement, 214

How Do Managers Plan Production? 215
Design Planning, 215 • Site Selection and Facilities Planning, 216

Sustain the Planet: Saving Energy—And the Environment 217
Operational Planning, 219

Operations Control 220
Purchasing, 220 • Inventory Control, 221 • Scheduling, 221 • Quality Control, 222

Personal Apps: Nobody likes complaints! 224
Production Planning: A Summary, 224

Improving Productivity with Technology 225
Productivity Trends, 225 • Improving Productivity Growth, 225 • The Impact of Automation, Robotics, and Computers on Productivity, 226 • Sustainability and Technological Displacement, 228

Summary 229

Key Terms 230

Discussion Questions 230

Test Yourself 231

Video Case: Chobani Gives the World a Taste for Greek Yogurt 232

Building Skills for Career Success 233

Running a Business: Part 3: Graeter's Grows Through Good Management, Organization, and Quality 234

Building a Business Plan: Part 3 236

Endnotes 237

PART 4 Human Resources 238

Chapter 9: **Attracting and Retaining the Best Employees 238**

→ **Inside Business:** Google Grows Through People Power 239

Human Resources Management: An Overview 239

Personal Apps: How many skills do you have? 240
HRM Activities, 240 • Responsibility for HRM, 240

Human Resources Planning 241
Forecasting Human Resources Demand, 241 • Forecasting Human Resources Supply, 241 • Matching Supply with Demand, 242

Cultural Diversity in Human Resources 243

Striving for Success: What Does a Chief Diversity Officer Do? 243

Job Analysis 245

Recruiting, Selection, and Orientation 246
Recruiting, 246 • Selection, 247 • Orientation, 249

Compensation and Benefits 249
   Compensation Decisions, 249 • *Comparable Worth, 250*

Personal Apps: Focus on what you can offer! 251
   Types of Compensation, 251 • *Employee Benefits, 251*

Training and Development 252

Social Media: Nuts About Southwest 253
   Analysis of Training Needs, 253 • *Training and Development Methods, 253* • *Evaluation of Training and Development, 254*

Performance Appraisal 254
   Common Evaluation Techniques, 254 • *Performance Feedback, 256*

The Legal Environment of HRM 257
   National Labor Relations Act and Labor–Management Relations Act, 257 • *Fair Labor Standards Act, 257* • *Equal Pay Act, 257* • *Civil Rights Acts, 257* • *Age Discrimination in Employment Act, 258* • *Occupational Safety and Health Act, 258* • *Employee Retirement Income Security Act, 259* • *Affirmative Action, 259* • *Americans with Disabilities Act, 259*

Summary 260

Key Terms 261

Discussion Questions 261

Test Yourself 262

Video Case: The Container Store Hires Great Employees to Sell Empty Boxes 263

   Building Skills for Career Success 264

Endnotes 265

Chapter 10: Motivating and Satisfying Employees and Teams 266

   → **Inside Business:** Satisfied Employees Help Create Satisfied Customers at American Express 267

What Is Motivation? 267

Historical Perspectives on Motivation 268
   Scientific Management, 268 • *The Hawthorne Studies, 269* • *Maslow's Hierarchy of Needs, 270* • *Herzberg's Motivation–Hygiene Theory, 271* • *Theory X and Theory Y, 273* • *Theory Z, 274* • *Reinforcement Theory, 274*

Personal Apps: What motivates you? 275

Contemporary Views on Motivation 275
   Equity Theory, 275 • *Expectancy Theory, 276*

Striving for Success: The Gamification of Motivation 276
   Goal-Setting Theory, 277

Key Motivation Techniques 278
   Management by Objectives, 278 • *Job Enrichment, 279* • *Behavior Modification, 280* • *Flextime, 280* • *Part-Time Work and Job Sharing, 281* • *Telecommuting, 282* • *Employee Empowerment, 282*

Sustain the Planet: Cash for Conservation? 282
   Employee Ownership, 283

Teams and Teamwork 284
   What Is a Team? 284 • *Types of Teams, 284* • *Developing and Using Effective Teams, 286* • *Roles Within a Team, 286*

Personal Apps: Is your team virtual? 287
   Team Cohesiveness, 287 • *Team Conflict and How to Resolve It, 287* • *Benefits and Limitations of Teams, 287*

Summary 288

Key Terms 289

Discussion Questions 289

Test Yourself 290

Video Case: Putting the Focus on People at the Fruit Guys 291

   Building Skills for Career Success 292

Running a Business: Part 4: At Graeter's, Tenure Is "a Proud Number" 293

Building a Business Plan: Part 4 295

Endnotes 296

PART 5   Marketing   297

© ANDY DEAN PHOTOGRAPHY/SHUTTERSTOCK.COM

Chapter 11: Building Customer Relationships Through Effective Marketing 297

   → **Inside Business:** Volkswagen: Eternally Trying to be the "People's Car" 298

Managing Customer Relationships 298

Ethical Success or Failure? The Customer Is Always Right—or Not 300

Utility: The Value Added by Marketing 300

The Marketing Concept 302
   Evolution of the Marketing Concept, 302 • *Implementing the Marketing Concept, 303*

Personal Apps: Think about the purchases you've made this year 303

Markets and Their Classification 303

Developing Marketing Strategies 304
   Target Market Selection and Evaluation, 304 • *Creating a Marketing Mix, 307*

Marketing Strategy and the Marketing Environment 309

Developing a Marketing Plan 309

Market Measurement and Sales Forecasting 310

Marketing Information 311
   Marketing Information Systems, 311 • *Marketing Research, 311*

Personal Apps: Tell us your thoughts 312
   Using Technology to Gather and Analyze Marketing Information, 312

Striving for Success: Using Neuroscience for Marketing Research 313

Types of Buying Behavior 314
   Consumer Buying Behavior, 314 • *Business Buying Behavior, 316*

Summary 316

Key Terms 318

Discussion Questions 318

Test Yourself 318

Video Case: Raleigh Wheels Out Steel Bicycle Marketing 320

   Building Skills for Career Success 320

Endnotes 321

Chapter 12: **Creating and Pricing Products That Satisfy Customers 322**

→ **Inside Business:** Thinking Outside the Box at Oreo 323

Classification of Products 324

   Consumer Product Classifications, 324 • Business Product Classifications, 325

The Product Life-Cycle 325

   Stages of the Product Life-Cycle, 325

Personal Apps: Do you have one of these? 327

   Using the Product Life-Cycle, 328

Product Line and Product Mix 328

Managing the Product Mix 329

   Managing Existing Products, 329 • Deleting Products, 330 • Developing New Products, 330

Entrepreneurial Success: Go Ahead, Write on the Walls! 332

   Why Do Products Fail? 332

Branding, Packaging, and Labeling 333

   What Is a Brand? 333 • Types of Brands, 333

Personal Apps: What's your favorite brand? 334

   Benefits of Branding, 334 • Choosing and Protecting a Brand, 335

Social Media: Social Networking for Success: Small Businesses Turn to Social Media for Effective Marketing 336

   Branding Strategies, 336 • Brand Extensions, 337 • Packaging, 337 • Labeling, 338

Pricing Products 339

   The Meaning and Use of Price, 339 • Price and Non-Price Competition, 339 • Buyers' Perceptions of Price, 340

Pricing Objectives 340

   Survival, 340 • Profit Maximization, 341 • Target Return on Investment, 341 • Market-Share Goals, 341 • Status-Quo Pricing, 341

Pricing Methods 341

   Cost-Based Pricing, 341 • Demand-Based Pricing, 342 • Competition-Based Pricing, 343

Pricing Strategies 344

   New-Product Pricing, 344 • Differential Pricing, 344 • Psychological Pricing, 345 • Product-Line Pricing, 346 • Promotional Pricing, 347

Pricing Business Products 347

   Geographic Pricing, 348 • Transfer Pricing, 348 • Discounting, 348

Summary 349

Key Terms 350

Discussion Questions 351

Test Yourself 351

Video Case: From Artistic Roots, Blu Dot Styles Marketing Strategy 353

   Building Skills for Career Success 353

Endnotes 354

Chapter 13: **Distributing and Promoting Products 356**

→ **Inside Business:** How Dick's Sporting Goods Captures the Category 357

Distribution Channels and Market Coverage 357

   Commonly Used Distribution Channels, 358

Personal Apps: Got water to drink? 360

   Level of Market Coverage, 360

Partnering Through Supply-Chain Management 360

Marketing Intermediaries: Wholesalers 361

   Wholesalers Provide Services to Retailers and Manufacturers, 361 • Types of Wholesalers, 361

Marketing Intermediaries: Retailers 362

   Types of Retail Stores, 363 • Types of Nonstore Selling, 365

Personal Apps: Where do you shop? 367

   Types of Shopping Centers, 367

Physical Distribution 368

   Inventory Management, 368 • Order Processing, 368 • Warehousing, 369 • Materials Handling, 369 • Transportation, 369

Sustain the Planet: Green Logistics 370

What Is Integrated Marketing Communications? 371

The Promotion Mix: An Overview 372

Advertising 373

   Types of Advertising by Purpose, 373 • Major Steps in Developing an Advertising Campaign, 374

Entrepreneurial Success: Via Ad Agency 376

   Advertising Agencies, 376 • Social and Legal Considerations in Advertising, 377

Personal Selling 377

   Kinds of Salespersons, 377 • The Personal-Selling Process, 378 • Major Sales Management Tasks, 379

Sales Promotion 379

   Sales Promotion Objectives, 379 • Sales Promotion Methods, 380 • Selection of Sales Promotion Methods, 380

Public Relations 382

   Types of Public-Relations Tools, 382 • Uses of Public Relations, 383

Summary 383

Key Terms 385

Discussion Questions 385

Test Yourself 386

Video Case: L.L.Bean Employs a Variety of Promotion Methods to Communicate with Customers 387

   Building Skills for Career Success 388

Running a Business: Part 5: Graeter's Is "Synonymous with Ice Cream" 390

Building a Business Plan: Part 5 392

Endnotes 393

Chapter 14: Exploring Social Media and e-Business 394

→ **Inside Business:** Domino's Puts e-Business and Social Media on the Menu 395

Why Is Social Media Important? 395
What Is Social Media and How Popular Is It? 396 • Why Businesses Use Social Media, 397

Personal Apps: Why Businesses "Like" Social Media 398

Social Media Tools For Business Use 398
Business Use of Blogs, 398 • Photos, Videos, and Podcasts, 399 • Social Media Ratings, 399 • Social Games, 400

Achieving Business Objectives Through Social Media 400
Social Media Communities, 400 • Crisis and Reputation Management, 401 • Listening to Stakeholders, 402 • Targeting Customers, 402 • Social Media Marketing, 403 • Generating New Product Ideas, 404 • Recruiting Employees, 405

Career Success: Make a Good Impression Using Social Media 405

Developing a Social Media Plan 406
Steps to Build a Social Media Plan, 406 • Measuring and Adapting a Social Media Plan, 408 • The Cost of Maintaining a Social Media Plan, 410

Defining e-Business 410
Organizing e-Business Resources, 410 • Satisfying Needs Online, 411 • Creating e-Business Profit, 412

Entrepreneurial Success: Starting an Online Farmers' Market 412

Personal Apps: What Do e-Businesses Sell? 413

Fundamental Models of e-Business 413
Business-to-Business (B2B) Model, 413 • Business-to-Consumer (B2C) Model, 415

The Future of the Internet, Social Media, and e-Business 416
Internet Growth Potential, 416 • Ethical and Legal Concerns, 416 • Future Challenges for Computer Technology, Social Media, and e-Business, 417

Summary 419

Key Terms 421

Discussion Questions 421

Test Yourself 421

Video Case: Luke's Lobster: Entrepreneurs Use Social Networking to Claw Their Way Up the Food Chain 423

Building Skills for Career Success 424

Endnotes 424

Chapter 15: Using Management and Accounting Information 426

→ **Inside Business:** Intuit Takes Technology into the Future 427

How Can Information Reduce Risk When Making a Decision? 428
Information and Risk, 428

Personal Apps: More Knowledge = Better Decisions 429
Information Rules, 429 • The Difference Between Data and Information, 429 • Knowledge Management, 430

What Is a Management Information System? 430
A Firm's Information Requirements, 430 • Costs and Limits of the System, 431

How Do Employees Use a Management Information System? 432
Step 1: Collecting Data, 432 • Step 2: Storing Data, 433 • Step 3: Updating Data, 433

Ethical Success or Failure? How Much Should Businesses Know About Internet Users? 434
Step 4: Processing Data, 434 • Step 5: Presenting Information, 434 • Making Smart Decisions, 435 • Business Application Software, 437

Why Accounting Information Is Important 437
Why Audited Financial Statements Are Important? 438 • Accounting Fraud, Ethical Behavior, and Reform, 439 • Different Types of Accounting, 440 • Careers in Accounting, 440

The Accounting Equation and the Balance Sheet 441
The Accounting Equation, 441 • The Balance Sheet, 442 • Assets, 442

Personal Apps: Smart Career Moves 445
Liabilities and Owners' Equity 445

The Income Statement 446
Revenues, 447

Entrepreneurial Success: Accounting for First-Time Entrepreneurs 448
Cost of Goods Sold, 448 • Operating Expenses, 448 • Net Income, 449

The Statement of Cash Flows 449

Evaluating Financial Statements 450
Comparing Financial Data, 451 • Financial Ratios, 452

Summary 453

Key Terms 455

Discussion Questions 455

Test Yourself 455

Video Case: Making the Numbers or Faking the Numbers? 457

Building Skills for Career Success 458

Endnotes 459

Chapter 16: Mastering Financial Management 460

→ **Inside Business:** How Cisco Finances Future Growth 461

Why Financial Management? 461
The Need for Financial Management, 462 • Financial Reform After the Economic Crisis, 463 • Careers in Finance, 463

The Need for Financing 464
Short-Term Financing, 464

Personal Apps: Do You Have a Financial Plan? 466
Long-Term Financing, 466 • The Risk–Return Ratio, 466

Planning—The Basis of Sound Financial Management, 467
Developing the Financial Plan, 467 • Monitoring and Evaluating Financial Performance, 469

Financial Services Provided by Banks and Other Financial Institutions 470
Traditional Banking Services for Business Clients, 470 • Why Has the Use of Credit Transactions Increased? 471 • Electronic Banking Services, 472 • International Banking Services, 473

Sources of Short-Term Debt Financing 473
Sources of Unsecured Short-Term Financing, 473 • Sources of Secured Short-Term Financing, 476 • Factoring Accounts Receivable, 476 • Cost Comparisons, 476

Sources of Equity Financing 477
Selling Stock, 477

Striving for Success: Investor Relations in the Social Media Era 479

Social Media: Talk to Chuck 480
Retained Earnings, 480 • Venture Capital and Private Placements, 480

Sources of Long-Term Debt Financing 481
Long-Term Loans, 481 • Corporate Bonds, 482

Personal Apps: You Are a CFO! 483
Cost Comparisons, 484

Summary 485

Key Terms 487

Discussion Questions 487

Test Yourself 487

Video Case: Financial Planning Equals Profits for Nederlander Concerts 489
Building Skills for Career Success 490

Running a Business: Part 6: Graeter's Recipe for Growth: New Systems, Social Media, and Financing 491

Building a Business Plan: Part 6 493

Endnotes 494

Answer Key   TY-1

Glossary   G-1

Name Index   NI-1

Subject Index   SI-1

The following appendixes appear on the companion site www.cengage.brain.com

Appendix A: Understanding Personal Finances and Investments   A-1

Appendix B: Careers in Business   B-1

Appendix C: Enhancing Union–Management Relations   C-1

Appendix D: Risk Management and Insurance   D-1

Appendix E: Business Law, Regulation, and Taxation   E-1

About the Authors

William M. Pride Texas A&M University

William M. Pride is professor of marketing, Mays Business School at Texas A&M University. He received his PhD from Louisiana State University. He is the author of Cengage Learning's *Marketing*, 15th edition, and a market leader. Dr. Pride's research interests are in advertising, promotion, and distribution channels. His research articles have appeared in major journals in the fields of advertising and marketing, such as *Journal of Marketing, Journal of Marketing Research, Journal of the Academy of Marketing Science*, and the *Journal of Advertising*. Dr. Pride is a member of the American Marketing Association, Academy of Marketing Science, Association of Collegiate Marketing Educators, Society for Marketing Advances, and the Marketing Management Association. He has taught principles of marketing and other marketing courses for more than 30 years at both the undergraduate and graduate levels.

Robert J. Hughes Richland College, Dallas County Community Colleges

Robert J. Hughes (PhD, University of North Texas) specializes in business administration and college instruction. He has taught Introduction to Business for more than 35 years both on campus and online for Richland College—one of the seven campuses that are part of the Dallas County Community College District. In addition to *Business* and *Foundations of Business*, published by Cengage Learning, he has authored college textbooks in personal finance and business mathematics; served as a content consultant for two popular national television series, *It's Strictly Business* and *Dollars & Sense: Personal Finance for the 21st Century*; and is the lead author for a business math project utilizing computer-assisted instruction funded by the ALEKS Corporation. He is also active in many academic and professional organizations and has served as a consultant and investment advisor to individuals, businesses, and charitable organizations. Dr. Hughes is the recipient of three different Teaching in Excellence Awards at Richland College. According to Dr. Hughes, after 35 years of teaching Introduction to Business, the course is still exciting: "There's nothing quite like the thrill of seeing students succeed, especially in a course like Introduction to Business, which provides the foundation for not only academic courses, but also life in the real world."

Jack R. Kapoor College of DuPage

Jack R. Kapoor (EdD, Northern Illinois University) is professor of business and economics in the Business and Technology Division at the College of DuPage, where he has taught Introduction to Business, Marketing, Management, Economics, and Personal Finance since 1969. He previously taught at Illinois Institute of Technology's Stuart School of Management, San Francisco State University's School of World Business, and other colleges. Professor Kapoor was awarded the Business and Services Division's Outstanding Professor Award for 1999–2000. He served as an Assistant National Bank Examiner for the U.S. Treasury Department and as an international trade consultant to Bolting Manufacturing Co., Ltd., Mumbai, India.

He is known internationally as a coauthor of several textbooks, including *Foundations of Business*, 3rd edition (Cengage Learning), has served as a content consultant for the popular national television series *The Business File: An Introduction to Business*, and developed two full-length audio courses in business and personal finance. He has been quoted in many national newspapers and magazines, including *USA Today, U.S. News & World Report*, the *Chicago Sun-Times, Crain's Small Business*, the *Chicago Tribune*, and other publications.

Dr. Kapoor has traveled around the world and has studied business practices in capitalist, socialist, and communist countries.

SUCCESS

Acknowledgments

The quality of this book and its supplements program has been helped immensely by the insightful and rich comments of a special set of instructors. Their thoughtful and helpful comments had real impact in shaping the final product. In particular, we wish to thank:

John Adams,
  San Diego Mesa College
Ken Anglin,
  Minnesota State University,
  Mankato
Ellen A. Benowitz,
  Mercer County Community
  College
Michael Bento,
  Owens Community College
Patricia Bernson,
  County College of Morris
Laura Bulas,
  Central Community College, NE
Brennan Carr,
  Long Beach City College
Paul Coakley,
  The Community College of
  Baltimore County
Jean Condon,
  Mid-Plains Community College
Mary Cooke,
  Surry Community College
Dean Danielson,
  San Joaquin Delta College
John Donnellan,
  Holyoke Community College
Gary Donnelly,
  Casper College
Karen Edwards,
  Chemeketa Community College
Donna K. Fisher,
  Georgia Southern University
Charles R. Foley,
  Columbus State Community
  College
Mark Fox,
  Indiana University South Bend
Connie Golden,
  Lakeland Community College
Karen Gore,
  Ivy Tech Community College—
  Evansville

Carol Gottuso,
  Metropolitan Community College
John Guess,
  Delgado Community College
Frank Harber,
  Indian River State College
Linda Hefferin,
  Elgin Community College
Tom Hendricks,
  Oakland Community College
Chip Izard,
  Richland College
Eileen Kearney,
  Montgomery Community College
Anita Kelley,
  Harold Washington College
Mary Beth Klinger,
  College of Southern Maryland
Natasha Lindsey,
  University of North Alabama
Robert Lupton,
  Central Washington University
John Mago,
  Anoka Ramsey Community
  College
Rebecca J. Mahr,
  Western Illinois University
Pamela G. McElligott,
  St. Louis Community College
  Meramec
Myke McMullen,
  Long Beach City College
Carol Miller,
  Community College of Denver
Jadeip Motwani,
  Grand Valley State
Mark Nagel,
  Normandale Community College
Dyan Pease,
  Sacramento City College
Jeffrey D. Penley,
  Catawba Valley Community
  College

Angela J. Rabatin,
  Prince George's Community College
Anthony Racka,
  Oakland Community College—
  Auburn Hills Campus
Dwight Riley,
  Richland College
Kim Rocha,
  Barton College
Carol Rowey,
  Community College of Rhode
  Island
Christy Shell,
  Houston Community College
Cindy Simerly,
  Lakeland Community College
Yolanda I. Smith,
  Northern Virginia Community
  College
Gail South,
  Montgomery College
Rieann Spence-Gale,
  Northern Virginia Comm.
  College—Alexandria Campus
Kurt Stanberry,
  University of Houston, Downtown
John Striebich,
  Monroe Community College
Keith Taylor,
  Lansing Community College
Tricia Troyer,
  Waubonsee Community College
Leo Trudel,
  University of Maine—Fort Kent
Randy Waterman,
  Richland College
Leslie Wiletzky,
  Pierce College—Ft. Steilacoom
Anne Williams,
  Gateway Community College

We also wish to acknowledge Colette Wolfson and Linda Hoffman of Ivy Tech Community College for their contributions to the *Instructor's Resource Manual*, as well as Julie Boyles of Portland State University for her help in developing the Test Bank. We thank Instructional Designer, Tiana Tagami, and ANSR Source for their excellent work on the PowerPoint program. For our CengageNOW and CourseMate content, we would again like to thank Julie Boyles as well as LuAnn Bean of the Florida Institute of Technology, Amit Shah of Frostburg State University, and ANSR Source. We thank the Dallas Center for Distance Learning Solutions for their Telecourse partnership and for providing the related student and instructor materials. Finally, we thank the following people for their professional and technical assistance: Stacy Landreth Grau, Marian Wood, Amy Ray, Elisa Adams, Jennifer Jackson, Jamie Jahns, Eva Tweety, Carolyn Phillips, Laurie Marshall, Clarissa Means, Theresa Kapoor, David Pierce, Kathryn Thumme, Margaret Hill, Nathan Heller, Karen Tucker, and Dave Kapoor.

Many talented professionals at Cengage Learning have contributed to the development of *Foundations of Business, 4e*. We are especially grateful to Erin Joyner, Mike Schenk, Jason Fremder, Kristen Hurd, Joanne Dauksewicz, Darrell Frye, Stacy Shirley, Kristen Meere, and Megan Fischer. Their inspiration, patience, support, and friendship are invaluable.

W. M. P.

R. J. H

J. R. K

Advisory Board
Pride/Hughes/Kapoor, FOUNDATIONS OF BUSINESS, 3e
(Conducted in-depth reviews, attended focus groups, responded to quick mini-surveys)

Michael Bento
Owens Community College
Patricia Bernson
County College of Morris
Brennan Carr
Long Beach City College
Paul Coakley
The Community College of Baltimore County
Donna K. Fisher
Georgia Southern University
Charles R. Foley
Columbus State Community College
Connie Golden
Lakeland Community College
John Guess
Delgado Community College
Frank Harber
Indian River State College

Anita Kelley
Harold Washington College
Mary Beth Klinger
College of Southern Maryland
Pamela G. McElligott
St Louis Community College Meramec
Mark Nagel
Normandale Community College
Angela J. Rabatin
Prince George's Community College
Anthony Racka
Oakland Community College— Auburn Hills Campus
Carol Rowey
Community College of Rhode Island
Christy Shell
Houston Community College

Cindy Simerly
Lakeland Community College
Yolanda I. Smith
Northern Virginia Community College
Gail South
Montgomery College
Rieann Spence-Gale
Northern Virginia Community College—Alexandria Campus
Kurt Stanberry
University of Houston, Downtown
John Striebich
Monroe Community College
Keith Taylor
Lansing Community College
Tricia Troyer
Waubonsee Community College